I Almost Quit Today

And 99 Other Reasons Working for a Living Is Ridiculous (But Here We Are)

Copyright © 2026 by Innovation Consultants of DeKalb.
Written by Shermaine Perry-Knights.

ISBN 978-1-953518-52-1

No part of this book may be used or reproduced in any manner whatsoever without the prior written permission of the author.

Read This First

You didn't fail. Work is just... a lot. This isn't a "how to climb the corporate ladder" book—it's a "how to survive without screaming into the void" book.

Look, if you picked this up, you're probably having one of those weeks. The kind where you fantasize about what your resignation email would say (you've written three drafts already). The kind where you calculate exactly how long you could survive on your savings if you just... stopped showing up. The kind where you wonder if anyone would actually notice if you joined that Zoom call with your camera off and just took a nap.

You're not alone. You're not dramatic. And no, you're not "just bad at adulting."

Work is weird and hard in ways nobody warned us about. They told us to follow our dreams and work hard, but they forgot to mention that Debra from HR would forward you passive-aggressive emails about "proper kitchen etiquette" or that your boss would use the phrase "circle back" seventeen times in one meeting.

This book isn't here to fix your job. (If I could do that, I'd be a billionaire.) It's here to remind you that you're not crazy, this is actually ridiculous, and sometimes the bravest thing you can do is make it through another Wednesday.

Read it in order. Skip around. Highlight the parts that make you laugh-cry. Use it as proof that you're not the only one who's ever hidden in a supply closet to avoid small talk.

You're going to be okay. Not today, maybe. Possibly not this week. But eventually.

For now, let's just survive this together.

How to Use This Book

Having a meltdown? Jump to Part 4 (Feelings Are Happening and You're Not Okay With It).

Your boss just said something that made you see red? Part 3 (The People Who Ruin Everything) is calling your name.

Wondering if you should quit or if you're just having a bad day? Part 6 (The Great "Should I Stay or Should I Go" Debate).

Just generally exhausted? Part 5 (The Myth of Balance) will validate your entire existence.

Need permission to feel your feelings? Literally any entry. That's the whole point.

This isn't homework. You won't be tested. There's no quiz at the end. You don't even have to agree with everything I say.

Think of this as advice from your friend who finally quit that toxic job and can now tell you the truth about everything. The one who gets it. The one who's definitely cried in a bathroom stall at least twice.

Grab a highlighter. Dog-ear pages. Write angry notes in the margins. Throw it across the room if you need to. This book can take it.

Just remember: You're tougher than your inbox wants you to believe. Now let's do this.

TABLE CONTENTS

1 Welcome to the Club Nobody Wanted to Join
"You're Not Losing It, This Is Actually Bananas"

2 The Lies We Swallowed Whole
"Work Hard, Follow Your Passion, and Other Fairy Tales"

3 The People Who Ruin Everything
"A Field Guide to Workplace Chaos Agents"

4 Feelings Are Happening and You're Not Okay With It
"The Emotional Chaos of Employment"

5 The Myth of Balance
"Work-Life What? When Your Job Wants Your Soul"

6 The Great "Should I Stay or Should I Go" Debate
"How to Tell If This Is a Bad Day or a Bad Life Choice"

7 Surviving When You Can't Leave (Yet)
"How to Not Lose Yourself While You're Stuck"

Bonus Section
Shit That Actually Helps (And Stuff That Doesn't)

Part 1: Welcome to the Club Nobody Wanted to Join

"You're Not Losing It, This Is Actually Bananas"

1. Congratulations, You're Normal

If you've ever:
- Sat in your car for an extra ten minutes before going inside because you Just. Couldn't. Yet.
- Googled "how to fake your own death and start over" during a meeting
- Felt your soul leave your body when your boss said "quick question"
- Wondered if everyone else got a manual you didn't receive
- Refreshed job postings while pretending to work
- Thought "I could just... not go back" and then gone back anyway

Welcome. You're one of us now.

The "I Almost Quit Today" club has no membership fees, no secret handshake, and the only requirement is that you've ever whispered "I hate it here" during a video call you thought was muted (but weren't 100% sure).

You're not broken. You're not failing. You're just a regular human trying to survive a system designed by people who apparently never needed to sleep, eat, or have feelings.

Population: Everyone who's ever had a job.

You're in excellent company.

2. Nobody Warned You About the Weird Parts

They prepared you for interviews. Resumes. "Professional communication."

But nobody mentioned that you'd develop an irrational hatred of the sound of Slack notifications. Or that you'd have a Pavlovian stress response to the phrase "per my last email."

Nobody told you that "team building exercises" means "forced fun with people you wouldn't hang out with voluntarily" or that "we're like a family" means "we're going to emotionally manipulate you into working late."

Nobody prepared you for how many hours of your life you'd spend in meetings that accomplish absolutely nothing. Or that you'd become fluent in Corporate Speak, a language where "let's take this offline" means "stop talking" and "synergy" means "I have no idea what I'm saying."

And nobody-nobody-warned you that you'd spend a solid 30% of your workday just pretending to look busy. If you feel blindsided, that's because you were sold a very sanitized version of employment. The reality is weirder. And that's not your fault.

3. The Sunday Scaries Are a Legit Medical Condition (Probably)

It's 3 PM on Sunday and your chest just got tight for no reason. Oh wait. There IS a reason. Tomorrow is Monday.

The Sunday Scaries aren't just "not wanting the weekend to end." They're full-body existential dread. It's your stomach dropping when you remember you have to go back. Back to the emails that never stop. Back to pretending you care about quarterly metrics. Back to Dave's unsolicited opinions about literally everything.

And here's the part that makes you feel like garbage: You feel guilty for feeling this way.
"Other people have it worse."
"At least I have a job."
"I'm being dramatic."

But if every single Sunday feels like preparing for battle, that's your body trying to tell you something. Maybe the job is wrong. Maybe you're burned out. Maybe the environment is toxic and you've just gotten really good at pretending it's normal. A little end-of-weekend sadness? Fine. Human. Relatable. But spending every Sunday evening filled with dread? That's a smoke alarm, friend. Don't ignore it.

4. "I'm Fine" (Narrator Voice: They Were Absolutely Not Fine)

Lies we tell to survive the workweek:
- "It's not that bad."
- "Everyone deals with this."
- "I just need to push through."
- "I'm probably being sensitive."
- "At least the benefits are good."

Recognize any of these?

Here's the truth bomb: You can acknowledge that it could be worse AND admit that it's currently bad.

Both things can exist at the same time. This isn't the Suffering Olympics. You don't need to earn the worst situation to be allowed to feel bad about yours.

You're allowed to be unhappy at work even if you have health insurance. You're allowed to be frustrated even if the pay is decent. You're allowed to want more even if other people would "kill for your position."

4. "I'm Fine" (Narrator Voice: They Were Absolutely Not Fine) continued

Pretending you're fine doesn't make you stronger. It just makes you really, really good at lying to yourself until you have a breakdown in the office bathroom.

So next time someone asks "How's work?" and you auto-respond with "Fine!", pause.

Are you actually fine? Or are you just performing fine because admitting the truth feels too vulnerable?

Because if you're reading this book, I'm betting on option two.

5. The Dream Job Is a Scam

Remember being a kid and adults asking what you wanted to be when you grew up?

You said "astronaut" or "marine biologist" or "person who gets paid to pet dogs" and they smiled and said you could be anything.

They lied. Kind of.

Not because those jobs don't exist, but because they forgot to mention that even your dream job comes with:
- Annoying coworkers
- Pointless meetings
- Bureaucratic nonsense
- Days when you'd rather be literally anywhere else
- Someone named Keith who microwaves fish

There is no magical perfect job where you wake up every single day excited to work. There's no career that will fulfill you 100% of the time without any frustration. There's no workplace where everything runs smoothly and everyone is lovely and you never want to fake your own death.

5. The Dream Job Is a Scam (continued)

Even people who love their jobs have bad weeks. Even people doing "meaningful work" get burnt out. Even people in their literal dream jobs sometimes Google "remote jobs in New Zealand" at 2 PM on a Tuesday.

So if you're waiting for the perfect job to swoop in and make everything better, I have bad news.

It doesn't exist.

What DOES exist? Jobs that are mostly tolerable. Jobs where you don't cry on the way there. Jobs that pay your bills without requiring your soul as collateral.

Lower your expectations. Seriously. You'll be so much happier.

6. You're Not Lazy, You're Just Running on Fumes

There's a voice in your head that sounds suspiciously like your worst boss combined with every "hustle culture" influencer on the internet.

It says things like:
- "Why can't you just get it together?"
- "Other people work harder and don't complain."
- "Maybe you're not cut out for this."
- "You're being lazy."

That voice is lying.

You're not lazy. Lazy is choosing not to do something you're fully capable of doing because you just don't feel like it. What you're experiencing is: burnout, decision fatigue, emotional exhaustion, your brain entering power-saving mode because you've been running on 2% battery for six months.

You're tired because you've been using all your energy just to appear functional. You're tired because small talk requires the emotional bandwidth of a TED Talk.

6. You're Not Lazy, You're Just Running on Fumes (continued)

You're tired because you've been in survival mode for so long your body forgot what "rest" means.

And no, you can't just "positive attitude" your way out of exhaustion. That's not how human bodies work.

Your brain is trying to protect you by shutting down non-essential functions. That's not weakness. That's biology.
So next time that voice tells you you're lazy, tell it to shut up. You're not lazy.

You're just tired. And honestly? Completely understandable.

7. One Bad Day Does Not Equal One Bad Life (Probably)

Hot take incoming: One terrible day doesn't mean your entire career is a disaster.

I know it doesn't feel that way when you're sitting at your desk at 10 AM, already counting down to 5 PM, wondering how you're going to survive seven more hours of this fresh hell.

In that moment, it feels permanent. Like this is your life now. Forever. This exact feeling. Until you retire at 87. But here's what's actually happening: You're having a bad day.

Maybe your boss was in a weird mood. Maybe you got critical feedback. Maybe Mercury is in retrograde. Maybe the coffee machine broke and you didn't have time for Starbucks and now you're operating on pure spite.

Who knows.

7. One Bad Day Does Not Equal One Bad Life (Probably) continued

The point is: This feeling—the "I cannot do this anymore" feeling—is temporary. Tomorrow might also suck. But it also might be fine. You won't know until you get there.

Before you spiral into full existential crisis mode, ask yourself:
- Is this a pattern or just a really bad moment?
- Will I care about this next week?
- Am I catastrophizing or is this legitimately as bad as it feels?

Sometimes you DO need to quit. Sometimes the job genuinely is terrible and you need an escape plan.

But sometimes? You just need to survive today. Order takeout. Watch something mind-numbing. Wake up tomorrow and try again. Don't make permanent decisions based on temporary feelings. (Unless the temporary feeling has been happening every day for eight months. Then it's not temporary. Then it's a pattern. Then we need to talk.)

8. Hard vs. Toxic (There's a Difference)

Not all difficult jobs are toxic. Sometimes work is just... hard. Here's the test.

Hard jobs:
- Push you to grow (even when you don't want to)
- Have challenging moments but also okay moments
- Leave you tired but not completely destroyed
- Have problems that can actually be solved
- Make you feel capable (eventually)
- Teach you things you didn't know before

Toxic jobs:
- Make you feel small on purpose
- Have way more bad days than decent days
- Leave you emotionally raw and possibly crying
- Have the same problems that never get fixed
- Make you question if you're competent at literally anything
- Teach you creative ways to hide in bathrooms

8. Hard vs. Toxic (There's a Difference)

If your job is hard but you're learning? That's growth. Uncomfortable? Yes. Normal? Also yes.

If your job makes you feel like you're slowly losing your grip on reality? That's not "paying your dues." That's toxicity wearing a professional blazer.

You're allowed to struggle with a hard job.

You are NOT required to tolerate a toxic one.
Learn the difference. It matters.

9. Your Mental Health Is Worth More Than the Paycheck

Read this until you believe it:
Your job is not worth your sanity.
Not the salary. Not the title. Not the fear of letting people down. Not the health insurance. Not the "but I've invested three years here."
Nothing is worth sacrificing your mental health for.
I know that's easier to say than to internalize, especially when rent exists and the job market is a nightmare. But staying somewhere that's actively destroying you isn't "being responsible."
It's just harm with a direct deposit.
You're not required to set yourself on fire to keep a corporation warm. You're not required to stay somewhere that's breaking you just because leaving feels scary.
If your job is making you anxious, depressed, physically ill, or unable to function like a normal human? You don't owe them another day. You don't owe them notice. You don't owe them a detailed exit interview.
You owe yourself a chance to feel okay again.
Everything else can be figured out.

10. The "At Least I Have a Job" Guilt Trip

You know what's exhausting?

Trying to guilt yourself into being grateful when you're actively miserable.

"At least I have a job."
"At least it pays my bills."
"At least I'm not unemployed."

Okay. Sure. AND it still sucks here.

Both can be true simultaneously. You can recognize that you're fortunate to have steady income AND acknowledge that your job is making you want to scream into a pillow for 47 consecutive hours.

Gratitude and dissatisfaction aren't mutually exclusive.

Telling yourself "other people have it worse" doesn't make your situation better. It just makes you feel bad for feeling bad, which is a terrible emotional hamster wheel to be stuck on.

So yes. Be grateful for stability and paychecks and healthcare.

10. The "At Least I Have a Job" Guilt Trip (continued)

But ALSO stop using gratitude as a weapon against yourself. Stop guilting yourself into staying somewhere that's hurting you.

You're allowed to want a job that doesn't make you cry on Tuesdays.

That's not ungrateful. That's called having standards.

11. "Just One More Year" Is a Trap

You told yourself you'd stay for one year. Build the resume. Get some experience. Save money. Then move on.

That was three years ago.

What happened?

You were too tired to job hunt. Or the market looked rough. Or you got a tiny raise that made leaving feel wasteful. Or you convinced yourself it wasn't "that bad."

And now "just one more year" has become your default setting.

Here's the uncomfortable part: **If you keep waiting for the "perfect time" to leave, you'll be waiting until retirement.**

There will ALWAYS be a reason to stay:
- A project that needs you
- A busy season coming up
- A bonus you don't want to miss
- A coworker who depends on you
- "Things might get better"

11. "Just One More Year" Is a Trap (continued)

But if you're staying out of inertia instead of intention, you're not being loyal. You're just scared.

Which-valid. Change is terrifying. The unknown is terrifying. Starting over is terrifying.

But you know what's also terrifying?

Waking up a decade from now and realizing you spent ten years being miserable because you were afraid to leave.

You don't have to quit tomorrow. But you DO have to stop lying to yourself about "just one more year."

One more year of what? Being unhappy? No thanks.

12. Permission to Have Zero Idea What You're Doing

You don't need a plan.

You don't need to know what's next. You don't need your entire future mapped out before you admit this job isn't working.

You're allowed to say: **"I don't know what I want, but I know it's not this."**

You're allowed to be confused. To change your mind. To have absolutely no idea what you're doing.

Most people don't have it figured out. They're just better at faking confidence.

So if you're waiting until you have all the answers before making a move, you're going to be waiting forever. Life doesn't work that way. Careers definitely don't. Sometimes you just have to trust that you'll figure it out as you go. You've done hard things before. You've survived 100% of your worst days so far. You'll get through this too.

You don't need a perfect plan. You just need to take the next step.

Part 2: The Lies We Swallowed Whole

"Work Hard, Follow Your Passion, and Other Fairy Tales"

13. "Do What You Love"
(Or: How to Ruin Your Hobbies)

"Do what you love and you'll never work a day in your life!" Cool. Cool cool cool. Counterpoint: Do what you love for money and you'll ruin the one thing that used to bring you joy.

Ask anyone who turned their hobby into a business. Ask the person who loved baking until they had to make 47 custom cakes for entitled customers who wanted a full wedding cake for $23. Ask the artist who now hates drawing because they've spent six months doing corporate logo designs.

Here's the thing about turning passion into profit: Work is still work. Even if you love your job, you still have deadlines. Difficult clients. Boring administrative tasks. Days when you wake up and absolutely do not want to do the thing you supposedly love.

And here's the really messed up part of this advice: It makes you feel like a failure if you're not obsessed with your job. Like, if you're not waking up every morning thrilled to work, you must have chosen wrong. You must be doing life incorrectly.

13. "Do What You Love"
(Or: How to Ruin Your Hobbies) (continued)

But most people aren't passionate about their jobs. Most people are just trying to pay rent without wanting to scream.

And that's okay. That's NORMAL. That's not a character flaw.

You don't have to love your job. You don't even have to like it most days. You just have to tolerate it long enough to fund the parts of your life that actually matter.
That's not settling. That's being realistic.

14. "Hard Work Pays Off" (Except When It Doesn't)

We've been fed this line our entire lives: Work hard and you'll be rewarded. Effort equals results. Dedication leads to success.

Then you enter the workforce and discover: LOL, no.

You work your ass off and watch someone else get promoted because they golf with the CEO. You stay late every night for six months and get the same 2% raise as the guy who leaves at 4:30 PM every day. You go above and beyond and your reward is... more work. Congratulations.

Because here's the secret they don't tell you: Hard work is the bare minimum.

It's not special. It's expected. It's not going to make you stand out. You know what gets rewarded? Being visible. Being likable. Knowing how to play the game. Being in the right Zoom room at the right time.

And yeah, that's annoying. It's unfair. It's demoralizing.

14. "Hard Work Pays Off" (Except When It Doesn't) (continued)

But once you understand that hard work alone won't save you, you can stop killing yourself trying to prove your worth through sheer exhaustion. Work smart. Build relationships. Advocate for yourself. Know when to say no.

Because burning yourself out to prove you're "dedicated"? That's not ambition.

That's just playing into a system designed to exploit you.

15. "Fake It Till You Make It" (Or Until You Break)

This advice sounds empowering until you realize it's just gaslighting yourself.

Yes, confidence matters. Yes, sometimes you have to do things that scare you. Yes, growth happens outside your comfort zone.

But "fake it till you make it" has morphed into "ignore every warning sign until you collapse in a Target parking lot." You can't fake your way out of burnout. You can't fake your way out of a toxic workplace. You can't fake your way out of a job that's fundamentally destroying you.

At some point, the mask cracks. And when it does, it's messy. So instead of faking it, try this revolutionary concept: Be honest about where you are.

"I don't know how to do this yet, but I'm learning." "I'm struggling and I need help." "This isn't working for me." Authenticity isn't weakness. Pretending everything is fine when you're drowning? THAT'S what breaks you.
Fake confidence for a scary presentation? Sure. Fine.
Fake being okay for months on end? Hard pass.

16. "You Have to Pay Your Dues"
(Translation: Suffer Because We Did)

"Paying your dues" is code for "we had it bad, so you should too."

It's become the excuse for:
- Underpaying people
- Overworking people
- Normalizing toxic behavior
- Accepting terrible treatment

"Oh, you're exhausted? We all were at your age. Suck it up."

No. Actually, you don't have to.

Just because previous generations normalized suffering doesn't mean you have to accept it. Just because "that's how it's always been" doesn't make it okay.

You don't have to stay at a job that treats you poorly to prove you're "serious." You don't have to work 70-hour weeks to show you're "committed." You don't have to tolerate disrespect because you're "entry-level."

16. "You Have to Pay Your Dues" (Translation: Suffer Because We Did) (conntinued)

Paying your dues should mean: learning, growing, gaining experience.

Not: suffering for the sake of suffering.

If someone tells you that you have to tolerate mistreatment because "that's just how it is," they're telling on themselves.

They survived a broken system and instead of trying to fix it, they're defending it.

You don't have to play along.

16. "You Have to Pay Your Dues" (Translation: Suffer Because We Did)

Paying your dues should mean: learning, growing, gaining experience.

Not: suffering for the sake of suffering.

If someone tells you that you have to tolerate mistreatment because "that's just how it is," they're telling on themselves.

They survived a broken system and instead of trying to fix it, they're defending it. You don't have to play along.

17. "It'll Look Good on Your Resume" (So Will Therapy)

Every time you're asked to:
- Take on extra unpaid work
- Stay late for the third time this week
- Sacrifice your weekend for "the experience"

Someone hits you with: "It'll look good on your resume!" You know what else would look good on your resume? Not having a mental breakdown.

Here's the truth: Most of the stuff people tell you to do "for your resume" doesn't matter. Hiring managers don't care that you worked 80-hour weeks. They don't care that you sacrificed your health for a company that would replace you in 48 hours. They don't care that you were a "team player" who said yes to everything.

They care about skills. Results. Whether you can do the job. So stop letting people guilt-trip you into overworking yourself with vague promises about your future. Your resume is not worth your well-being. And honestly? A gap in employment is less concerning than burning out so hard you need six months to remember what joy feels like. Protect yourself. Your resume will be fine.

18. "We're Like a Family Here" (RUN)

When a workplace says "we're like a family," what they mean is:

- We'll guilt you into working unpaid overtime
- We'll expect work to be your #1 priority always
- We'll blur boundaries until you don't know where work ends and life begins
- We'll be deeply hurt if you set reasonable limits
- We'll call you "disloyal" if you leave for a better opportunity

Healthy workplaces don't call themselves families. They call themselves teams.

Teams have boundaries. Teams have roles. Teams don't require you to sacrifice everything. Real families love you unconditionally (ideally).

Work "families" love you as long as you're useful. So next time someone says "we're like a family here," smile and remember: Your real family wouldn't fire you for missing quarterly targets. This is a job. Treat it like one.

19. "Just Be Grateful" (The Ultimate Guilt Trip)

Ah yes. The favorite weapon of people who want you to stop complaining.

"Other people have it worse." "At least you're employed." "You should be grateful."

Cool. And also: Being grateful doesn't mean I can't want better.

You can appreciate having financial stability AND hate your job. You can be thankful for a paycheck AND still want to work somewhere that doesn't make you miserable. You can acknowledge your privilege AND advocate for yourself. Gratitude $\neq$ Complacency.

Telling someone to "just be grateful" is a manipulation tactic designed to make them feel guilty for having standards.

You're allowed to want a job that doesn't drain your will to live. That's not ungrateful. That's called self-respect. So next time someone hits you with this, try: "I AM grateful. I'm also allowed to want better. Both can be true."

Watch them short-circuit.

20. "Everyone Starts at the Bottom" (But How Long Do We Stay There?)

Sure, everyone starts at the bottom.

But "starting" implies movement. Progress. Eventually getting to NOT the bottom. Some workplaces love to keep people "at the bottom" indefinitely. They underpay you, overwork you, dangle vague "growth opportunities" that never materialize.

And when you finally advocate for yourself—ask for a raise, request a promotion, set a boundary—they hit you with: "Well, everyone starts at the bottom."

Yeah. Three years ago. If you've been "starting" for multiple years, you're not starting anymore. You're stuck. And that's not personal failure. That's a company taking advantage.

Starting at the bottom is fine. Staying there because your employer refuses to invest in your growth? That's exploitation. Don't let them gaslight you into thinking you're being impatient. You're not. You're recognizing that loyalty should be mutual. And if they're not investing in you, why are you still investing in them?

21. "Success Takes Sacrifice"
(But Not Your Entire Soul)

Yes, success requires trade-offs. But it shouldn't require everything.

There's this idea that if you want to be successful, you have to sacrifice:
- Your personal life
- Your hobbies
- Your relationships
- Your health
- Your sanity
- Your ability to enjoy literally anything

That if you're not exhausted, you're not working hard enough. That's not ambition. That's a cult. Real success is sustainable. It doesn't require destroying yourself in the process. It doesn't force you to choose between your career and your humanity.

And if your version of "success" is making you miserable, it's time to redefine what success means to you. Maybe success isn't a corner office. Maybe it's being able to enjoy dinner without checking your email. Maybe it's paying bills without panic. Maybe it's just... not hating your life.

21. "Success Takes Sacrifice" (But Not Your Entire Soul) (continued)

Stop letting hustle culture convince you that suffering is a requirement. You can be ambitious without being burnt out. You can work hard without working yourself into the ground.

Sacrifice is part of growth.

But it's not supposed to be your whole personality.

22. "Your Job Doesn't Have to Fulfill You" (True, But Also...)

This one is technically true. But let's add nuance.

Your job doesn't have to be your passion. It doesn't have to give your life meaning. It doesn't have to be the thing you're most proud of. Work is one part of your life. Not the entire thing.

HOWEVER. There's a difference between "not fulfilling" and "actively soul-crushing."

If your job is neutral—pays bills, doesn't stress you out excessively, leaves you energy for your actual life—great! Perfect! Gold star!

But if your job is draining every ounce of energy you have, leaving you with nothing for the things that DO matter? That's a problem.

You don't need to love your job. But you DO need to be able to tolerate it without it destroying you. Your job doesn't have to fulfill you. But it also shouldn't leave you completely empty. Find the balance.

23 "If You Can't Handle This, You Won't Make It Anywhere" (Gaslighting 101)

This is what toxic managers say when they don't want to fix their toxic behavior.

If someone tells you this, they're trying to convince you that YOU'RE the problem when actually THEY'RE the problem.

Truth: If you can't handle this specific dysfunctional workplace, it doesn't mean you can't handle ANY workplace. It means THIS PLACE SUCKS. Not every job is like yours. Not every boss is terrible. Not every company operates in chaos mode 24/7.

If you're struggling here, it doesn't mean you're weak. It means you're in an unsustainable environment. Don't let anyone gaslight you into thinking universal suffering is required for employment.

There are jobs where you won't feel like you're drowning constantly. There are workplaces where you won't question your competence daily. There are managers who won't make you cry. If you "can't handle this," good. That means you have standards. Don't lower them.

24. "It Gets Better" (Does It Though?)

Sometimes it does. You adjust, learn the systems, and things get easier. But sometimes "it gets better" is just something people say to get you to stop complaining. If you've been telling yourself "it'll get better" for six months and nothing has changed, it's not getting better.

You've just gotten better at tolerating dysfunction.

There's a difference between:
- Adjustment period discomfort
- Long-term systemic toxicity

If you're still miserable after giving it a legitimate shot, it's probably not going to magically improve. You're just getting more skilled at being miserable.

That's not growth. That's learned helplessness. Give things time, yes. But also trust yourself when you realize time isn't fixing anything.

It's okay to walk away from something that isn't improving. You're not giving up. You're redirecting your energy toward something that might actually be worth it.

Part 3: The People Who Ruin Everything

"A Field Guide to Workplace Chaos Agents"

25. The Micromanager
(Trust Issues in Human Form)

Identifying features:
- Needs to be CC'd on literally everything
- Checks in seven times before lunch
- Revises your perfectly fine work just to feel useful
- Hovers like you're about to commit workplace arson

Working for a micromanager is like having a helicopter parent, except you're 32 and she's not even your mom. It's not about your competence. It's about their control issues. They don't trust you because they don't trust anyone, including themselves, and instead of getting therapy they've made it your problem.

Survival tactics:
- Document EVERYTHING (so they can't claim you didn't do it)
- Overcommunicate proactively (beat them to the check-in)
- Set small boundaries ("I'll update you Friday EOD")
- Remember: This says nothing about you

You can't fix them. You can only manage around them. And if it becomes unbearable? Start job hunting. Micromanagers don't change. They just find new people to hover over.

26. The Credit Thief
(Also Known As: That Guy)

They take your ideas in meetings and present them as their own. They somehow always end up with their name on projects they barely touched. They magically reframe every "we did this" into "I did this" when talking to leadership.

The Credit Thief thrives in places where visibility matters more than actual work.

Survival tactics:
- Email your ideas BEFORE the meeting (creates a paper trail)
- Speak up fast in meetings before they can claim credit
- Loop leadership in on your work directly
- Stop helping them if they keep stealing

And if they DO steal credit? Call it out. Calmly. Professionally. But publicly.

"Thanks for sharing my idea! Next time, let's make sure we're both credited for our contributions."

Passive-aggressive? Maybe. Effective? Absolutely.

27. The Meeting Enthusiast
(Enemy of Calendars Everywhere)

This person's solution to everything is ANOTHER MEETING.

A question that could be answered in Slack? Meeting. An update nobody asked for? Meeting. A problem that could be solved via email? You guessed it—meeting.

Your calendar looks like a game of Tetris designed by someone who hates you.

Survival tactics:
- Politely decline meetings without clear agendas
- Suggest async alternatives ("Can we handle this over email?")
- Block "focus time" on your calendar (make it unmovable)
- Perfect the art of "Can this be an email?" (They'll hate you. Worth it.)

Your time is not infinite.

Protect it like your sanity depends on it. (It does.)

28. The Reply-All Bandit

Nobody—and I mean NOBODY—needs to see their "Thanks!" in an email chain with 100 people
.

Nobody cares about their out-of-office autoreply.

Nobody asked for their opinion on the company potluck theme.

And yet. Here we are.

Survival tactics:
- Mute the thread immediately
- Resist the urge to reply-all with "PLEASE STOP"
- Accept that some people will never learn
- Consider this free entertainment

This is not a battle worth fighting. Let it go.

(But also, if YOU'RE the Reply-All Bandit: Stop. We're begging you.)

29. The Work-Dumper
(Master of "Quick Favors")

"Hey, can you just handle this real quick?"

No. No, they cannot.

But they know you're a people-pleaser, so they keep asking. And you keep saying yes because you don't want to seem difficult or unhelpful.

And now you're doing two jobs while they... do whatever they do. (Honestly, unclear.)

Survival tactics:
- Start saying no (Revolutionary concept, I know)
- "I'd love to help, but I'm at capacity" is a complete sentence
- Stop rescuing them from their own bad planning
- Let them fail (They'll learn. Or they won't. Either way, not your circus)

You are NOT responsible for other people's workload.

Repeat it until you believe it: Not. Your. Problem.

30. The Indecisive Boss
(Master of "Pending")

Nothing is ever final. Everything is "TBD." They ask for your opinion and then completely ignore it. Or they change their mind six times before lunch.

You're stuck in permanent limbo, unable to move forward because they can't commit to literally anything.

Survival tactics:
- Get decisions in writing (so they can't backtrack)
- Set deadlines for feedback ("I need an answer by Friday or I'm proceeding with Option A")
- Make peace with ambiguity (or start job hunting)

Indecisive leaders create chaos.

You can't fix them. You can only protect yourself from the wreckage.

31. The Oversharer
(TMI Personified)

You know WAY too much about their personal life.

Their divorce details. Their medical procedures. Their Tinder disasters. Their ongoing feud with their neighbor about a tree.

You didn't ask. But they told you anyway. In detail. With visual aids.

Survival tactics:
- Headphones = universal "do not disturb" sign
- "I actually need to focus right now" works wonders
- Don't engage (The more you respond, the more they share)
- Remember: You're not their therapist

You can be friendly without being their emotional support coworker.

32. The Boss Who Plays Favorites (Fairness Not Included)

Some people can do no wrong. Others can do no right. And it has absolutely nothing to do with performance.

Golden Child gets promoted. You get more work.

Golden Child makes a mistake? "No big deal!" You make the same mistake? Disciplinary meeting.

Survival tactics:
- Document everything (protect yourself)
- Don't waste energy trying to win them over (You can't logic someone out of illogical favoritism)
- Build relationships with OTHER leaders
- Know when it's time to leave

Playing favorites is a sign of terrible leadership.

And you can't fix bad leadership from below.

33. The "Brutally Honest" Person (Actually Just Brutal)

"I'm just being honest."

No. You're being rude. There's a difference.

"Brutal honesty" is code for "I'm going to say something mean and act like it's YOUR fault for being sensitive."

Survival tactics:
- Call it out: "I don't think honesty requires cruelty"
- Disengage (Don't reward their behavior)
- Document if it crosses into harassment territory

Honesty without kindness is just cruelty with better PR.

34. The Perpetually "Busy" Person

They can't help with anything because they're "sooooo busy."

But they have time to:
- Scroll social media for 45 minutes
- Take two-hour lunches
- Stand in the break room complaining about how busy they are
- Participate in extended Slack conversations about The Bachelor

Survival tactics:
- Stop expecting help from them
- Let them drown in their imaginary urgency
- Focus your energy on people who actually contribute

Some people wear busyness like a medal.

Let them. You have actual work to do.

35. The Cryptic Slack Messenger

"Can we talk?"

"Call me when you get a chance."

"Need to discuss something."

NO CONTEXT. No urgency level. Just pure anxiety fuel.

Survival tactics:
- Respond with: "Sure! What's this regarding?"
- Stop assuming every vague message = bad news
- Ask for context upfront

If they wanted to fire you, they probably wouldn't Slack you about it first. Probably.

36. The Glory Hog

Team succeeds → They're the hero who saved everything

Team fails → Somehow everyone else's fault

Survival tactics:
- Speak up about your contributions early and often
- Don't let them rewrite history unchallenged
- Make your work visible to leadership directly

Recognition doesn't fall into your lap.

You have to claim it.

37. The 4:55 PM Friday Meeting Scheduler

This person has zero regard for anyone's time, sanity, or weekend plans.

They are chaos incarnate.

Survival tactics:
- Decline the meeting
- Block Friday afternoons on your calendar
- Suggest literally any other time
- Accept that they might be mad (Their problem, not yours)

Your weekend is non-negotiable.

Die on this hill.

Part 4: Feelings Are Happening and You're Not Okay With It

"The Emotional Chaos of Employment"

38. Welcome to Imposter Syndrome (Population: Everyone)

You feel like a fraud.

Like everyone else knows what they're doing and you're just winging it with increasingly creative bullshit.

Like someone's going to figure out you have no idea what you're talking about and escort you from the building.

Here's the secret nobody tells you: Everyone feels this way. Even the confident people. Even leadership. Even the person who just got promoted.

Imposter syndrome doesn't mean you're incompetent. It means you're self-aware enough to know you don't know everything. Which, honestly, is a good thing.

The people WITHOUT imposter syndrome? Usually the ones who should have it. The Venn diagram of "extreme confidence" and "actual competence" is not a circle.

39. You're Not Bad at Your Job, You're Just New at It

Being new = learning, making mistakes, asking questions, feeling uncertain

Being bad = not trying, not improving, ignoring feedback, showing up drunk

If you're worried about being bad at your job, you're probably fine.

People who are actually bad don't worry about it.

Give yourself time. You'll get there.

(Or you won't, and you'll pivot to something else. That's also fine.)

40. The Feedback That Absolutely Destroyed You

Not all feedback is created equal.

Some is constructive. Some is harsh. Some is just... mean. And when you're already feeling fragile, even GOOD feedback can feel like a personal attack on your entire existence.

How to survive:
- Take 24 hours before responding (Emotional reactions rarely help)
- Separate what's useful from what's unnecessarily cruel
- Ask for clarification if something's unclear
- Remember: Feedback is about your work, not your worth as a human

Bad feedback says more about the person giving it than about you.

(But also, if multiple people are giving you the same feedback, maybe listen.) Always remember that feedback is a gift, sometimes the gift that you don't really want but really need.

41. Burnout Isn't a Personality Trait

You're exhausted all the time. You can't focus on anything. You don't care anymore about things you used to care about. That's not dedication. That's burnout.

Signs you're burnt out:
- Everything feels impossible
- You're irritable with everyone (including people you actually like)
- Sleep is either impossible or all you want to do
- Things you used to enjoy feel like chores
- Your body is staging a revolt (headaches, stomach issues, etc.)

If this sounds familiar, you don't need better time management.

You need rest. Real rest. Not "I'll relax on Sunday" rest. Deep, sustained, guilt-free rest. Your body is screaming at you. Maybe listen?

42. Sunday Night Dread (A Weekly Tradition)

Sunday night isn't just "ugh, the weekend is ending."

It's:
- Lying awake thinking about everything you have to do
- Physical chest tightness as the hours pass
- Checking work email even though you KNOW you shouldn't
- Wishing you could call in sick but you're not actually sick

If this happens EVERY week, your body is sending you a message. Listen to it.

44. Anxiety Is a Liar

Your brain is CONVINCED everything is about to fall apart.

You're going to get fired. You're going to fail spectacularly. Everyone thinks you're incompetent.

But here's the thing: Anxiety is not a fact-checker.

It's your brain trying to protect you from worst-case scenarios that probably won't happen.

When anxiety spirals, ask yourself:
- Is this based on facts or feelings?
- What actual evidence do I have?
- Would I say this to a friend in the same situation?

Anxiety is loud.

But it's not always right.

45. The Mid-Meeting Panic Attack

Heart racing. Can't breathe. Need to leave but can't because you're in a meeting and everyone's staring at their screens but ALSO MAYBE AT YOU.

Quick grounding:
- 5 things you can see
- 4 things you can touch
- 3 things you can hear
- 2 things you can smell
- 1 thing you can taste

It won't make the panic disappear instantly, but it'll help you survive the next few minutes.

You're okay. It feels awful, but you're safe.

46. The Emotional Hangover

Yesterday was brutal. Today you feel... nothing. Numb. Drained. Like you can't handle anything at all.

That's an emotional hangover.

Just like a regular hangover, the cure is: rest, water, self-compassion, and time.

You're not lazy. You're recovering.

47. When You Lose It Over Something Tiny

You didn't cry about the deadline. You didn't cry about the criticism. You didn't cry about the passive-aggressive email.

You cried because the printer jammed.

That's burnout.

It's not the big things that break you. It's the tiny thing that happens when you're already at 100% capacity.

If you lose it over something small, it's not because you're dramatic.

It's because you're at your absolute limit.

48. Making Friends With Imposter Syndrome (Since It's Not Leaving)

You can't eliminate imposter syndrome.

But you CAN stop letting it run your life.

Next time it shows up: "Thanks for trying to protect me, brain. But I've got this."

Acknowledge it. Don't fight it.

Then do the thing anyway.

49. The Comparison Trap (Or: How to Feel Bad About Yourself in 30 Seconds)

Everyone else is getting promoted.

Everyone else has their life together.

Everyone else seems fine.

Except they're not.

You're comparing your behind-the-scenes mess to everyone else's highlight reel.

Stop it. You're doing better than you think.

50. You're Allowed to Have Feelings (Even at Work)

You're not a robot. You're not supposed to suppress every emotion.

You're allowed to be frustrated. Disappointed. Sad. Angry. Having feelings doesn't make you unprofessional.

It makes you human. Stop apologizing for being human.

Part 5: The Myth of Balance

"Work-Life What? When Your Job Wants Your Soul"

51. Work-Life Balance Is Fake

Let's just say it: Balance doesn't exist.

Some weeks, work takes over completely. Some weeks, you actually remember you have a life outside of spreadsheets.

The goal isn't achieving perfect 50/50 balance every single day. It's not letting work consume you EVERY SINGLE WEEK.

Stop aiming for balance. Aim for "sustainable chaos."

52. "Just One More Thing" Is a Complete Lie

Your boss at 4:45 PM: "Can you just do one more thing before you leave?"

Narrator: It was never just one thing.

Two hours later, you're still at your desk, wondering how "one quick email" turned into restructuring an entire project.

What to say next time: "I can tackle that first thing tomorrow morning!"

Then LEAVE.

You're not being difficult. You're protecting your sanity.

53. The Guilt of Leaving at 5 PM (When Everyone Else Is Still There)

Everyone else is still working.

If you leave, you'll look lazy. Uncommitted. Like you don't care.

So you stay. Even though you finished your work. Even though you're exhausted.

Here's your permission slip: Leave.

Staying late doesn't make you a better employee. It makes you an employee with no boundaries.

Leave at 5. Your work will still be there tomorrow. (Unfortunately.)

54. Why You Can't Stop Checking Your Email (Even on Vacation)

Even on your day off. Even at dinner. Even at 11 PM while you're supposed to be sleeping.

You tell yourself you're "just checking in."

But really? You're afraid. Afraid of missing something urgent. Afraid of seeming unresponsive. Afraid of coming back to 847 unread emails.

Radical idea: Delete work email from your phone.

I know. Revolutionary. But if you can't trust yourself not to check it, remove the temptation.

Your mental health > being the first to respond to Stacey's non-urgent question at 9 PM on Saturday.

55. Burnout Is Sneaky (Until It's Not)

Burnout doesn't announce itself.

It's gradual. Slow. You don't notice until you're in too deep.

First, you're just tired. Then you're exhausted. Then you're detached. Then you're numb. Then you're crying in your car before work wondering how you got here.

The fix: Catch it early. Rest before you're forced to.

Don't wait until you collapse.

56. Setting Boundaries Makes You Smart, Not Lazy

If you're saying no to extra projects, declining after-work drinks, or skipping the "optional but mandatory" team bonding event, you're not antisocial.

You're protecting your energy.

And that's not selfish. That's smart.

You can't pour from an empty cup. (Yes, it's cliché. It's also true.)

Truth by told, you shouldn't pour from a cup unless it's overflowing.

57. Your PTO Is Not a Suggestion

You have vacation time. USE IT.

Don't let it expire. Don't let them guilt you out of taking it. Don't "save it for later."

Later never comes.

You earned it. Take it. No explanation needed.

"I'm taking PTO" is a statement, not a request.

PTO= Prepare the others (respectfully, of course)

58. Stop Ruining Your Sunday With Work Prep

Spending Sunday night planning for the week, organizing your to-do list, pre-writing emails?

STOP.

Your Sunday is not a work day.

Let Monday be Monday. You'll deal with it when you get there.

Reclaim your weekend.

59. Boundaries Feel Impossible When You've Never Set Any

You've been a "yes" person your entire career.

Now you want to start saying no, and it feels terrifying. Like you're going to get fired for having limits.

Start small:
- "I can't take that on right now."
- "Let me check my workload and get back to you."
- "That doesn't work for me."

It gets easier with practice. Promise.

60. "Hustle Now, Rest Later" Is a Scam

You can't.

If you burn yourself out now, you won't be able to enjoy later.

Rest isn't a reward for productivity. It's a requirement for survival.

You're not a machine. You need downtime to function.

61. The Guilt of Doing Nothing

You've been conditioned to believe that productivity = worth.

That rest is lazy. That downtime is wasted time.

But you're not a robot. You need rest.

Stop feeling guilty for being human.

62. Work Expands to Fill the Time You Give It

If you're always available, work will always find you.

Set limits. Protect your time fiercely.

Or work will take everything—and then ask for more.

63. Your Job Is Part of Your Life, Not All of It

Your job is ONE part of your life.

You're allowed to have hobbies. Friends. Interests. A personality outside of your job title.

You don't owe your employer your entire existence.

Part 6: The Great "Should I Stay or Should I Go" Debate

"How to Tell If This Is a Bad Day or a Bad Life Choice"

64. Questions to Ask Before You Rage-Quit

Before you send that glorious resignation email, pause and ask:
- Is this a pattern or just a really bad week?
- Have I actually tried to fix it?
- Do I have a financial cushion to leave?
- What would make this job tolerable?
- Am I running toward something or away from something?

Don't make permanent decisions based on temporary rage.

(But also, if the rage has been happening for 8 months straight, it's not temporary.)

65. Red Flags You Cannot Ignore

Some things are non-negotiable dealbreakers:
- Your boss yells at you or belittles you
- You're being discriminated against or harassed
- The company does unethical/illegal things
- Your mental or physical health is suffering
- You're being asked to do something illegal

If ANY of these apply: Start planning your exit. Now.

66. When "Give It Six Months" Turns Into Three Years

You told yourself you'd give it six months to improve.

It's been three years.

At some point, you're not "giving it time." You're just scared to leave.

The question: When do you stop waiting for things to get better?

The answer: When you realize you're not waiting for improvement. You're waiting for courage.

67. The Job Won't Change. You Have To.

You can't fix a toxic workplace from the inside.

You can't make a bad boss suddenly care.

You can't force a company to value you.

The only thing you CAN control is whether you stay.

68. What If You Quit and Regret It?

Valid fear.

But also: What if you stay and regret THAT?

Both are possibilities. But only one lets you move forward.

69. Calculating the Real Cost of Staying

What is this job actually costing you?

- Your mental health?
- Your relationships?
- Your physical health?
- Your sense of self?
- Your weekends?
- Your ability to enjoy literally anything?

Sometimes the cost of staying is higher than the cost of leaving.

Do the math.

70. You Don't Need a New Job to Start Looking

Update your resume. Network. Apply to things. Talk to recruiters.

You don't have to quit tomorrow.

But you CAN start planning your exit today.

Having options makes everything feel less trapped.

71. When Good Benefits Aren't Enough

Health insurance is great. PTO is great. 401(k) match is great.

But none of that matters if the job is actively destroying you.

You can't enjoy benefits if you're too burnt out to function.

72. The Sunk Cost Fallacy (Or: Why "But I've Been Here Three Years" Doesn't Matter)

You've invested so much time here.

Three years. Or five. Or ten.

But that's not a reason to stay. That's the sunk cost fallacy.

You can't get that time back. But you CAN stop wasting more of it.

73. Permission to Walk Away

You don't need a "good enough" reason to leave.

"I'm miserable" IS a good enough reason.

You don't need to justify wanting better.

74. What If This Is As Good As It Gets?

It's not.

There are better jobs. Better managers. Better workplace cultures.

This isn't the only option, even when it feels like it is.

75. Quitting Isn't Giving Up

Quitting is redirecting your energy toward something that might actually be worth it.

That's not failure. That's wisdom.

76. Trust Your Gut

You know whether this job is fixable or not.

Deep down, you know.

Stop second-guessing yourself.

Listen to that voice.

Part 7: Surviving When You Can't Leave (Yet)

"How to Not Lose Yourself While You're Stuck"

77. When You're Stuck But Can't Keep Going Like This

You can't leave yet. Bills exist. The job market is rough. Timing is bad.

So now what?

You make it tolerable. You protect yourself. You survive strategically until you can escape.

78. Emotionally Detach (Without Becoming a Robot)

Stop caring so much.

Not about doing good work—still do your job well.

But stop investing emotionally in a place that doesn't invest in you.

It's just a job. Treat it like one.

79. The Boundaries You Can Actually Keep

You can't control your boss or your workload.

But you CAN control:
- When you check email
- Whether you work late
- How much you care
- How available you are

Start small. Protect what you can.

80. Find Meaning Outside of Work

If your job isn't fulfilling, find fulfillment elsewhere.

Hobbies. Relationships. Volunteering. Side projects. Literally anything that reminds you you're more than your job title.

Your job doesn't have to be your whole identity.

(In fact, it probably shouldn't be.)

81. Reframe Your Situation

"I'm stuck here" → "I'm choosing to stay while I plan my next move"

It's the same situation. But one gives you agency. Words matter.

82. Extract Value Before You Leave

What can you get out of this job while you're here?

Skills? Connections? Experience? References?

Use it. Learn what you can. Then bounce.

83. Stop Trying to Fix Things That Aren't Your Job

You can't fix the company culture.

You can't change your boss's personality.

You can't make your coworkers less annoying.

Focus on what you CAN control. Let everything else go.

84. Give Yourself a Timeline

"I'll stay six more months while I save money and job hunt."

Having an end date makes tolerating things SO much easier.

85. Protect Your Mental Health Like It's Your Full-Time Job

Because honestly? It kind of is.

Therapy. Exercise. Whatever keeps you sane.

Prioritize it. Schedule it. Protect it.

86. Coast Mode Is Allowed

You don't have to go above and beyond.

You can do the bare minimum, collect your paycheck, and go home.

You don't owe them your soul.

87. Remember Why You're Staying

Money. Experience. Timing. Health insurance.

Whatever it is, remind yourself regularly.

It's temporary. You have a plan.

88. You're Tougher Than You Think

You've survived 100% of your bad days so far.

That's a pretty good track record.

You'll survive this, too.

Bonus Section: Shit That Actually Helps (And Stuff That Doesn't)

89. THE REAL WORKPLACE GLOSSARY

QUICK TRANSLATIONS FOR THE CONFUSING LINGO ON THE JOB.

THE REAL WORKPLACE GLOSSARY

"WE'RE LIKE A FAMILY" = GUILT-TRIPPING COMING SOON

"FAST-PACED ENVIRONMENT" = ORGANIZED CHAOS (EMPHASIS ON CHAOS)

"WEAR MANY HATS" = DO THREE JOBS, GET PAID FOR ONE

"COMPETITIVE SALARY" = WE GOOGLED THE BARE MINIMUM

"FLEXIBLE SCHEDULE" = YOU'LL WORK AT ALL HOURS

THE REAL WORKPLACE GLOSSARY

"SELF-STARTER" = WE WON'T TRAIN YOU

"ROCK STAR" = WE WANT SOMEONE YOUNG AND EXPLOITABLE

SIDE HUSTLE — A SECOND JOB YOU JUSTIFY AS "CREATIVE FREEDOM."

"LET'S CIRCLE BACK" = I'M NEVER ADDRESSING THIS AGAIN

"SYNERGY" = I DON'T KNOW WHAT I'M TALKING ABOUT

THE REAL WORKPLACE GLOSSARY

"LET'S TAKE THIS OFFLINE" = STOP TALKING

"LOW-HANGING FRUIT" = EASY STUFF WE SHOULD'VE DONE ALREADY

SIDE HUSTLE — A SECOND JOB YOU JUSTIFY AS "CREATIVE FREEDOM."

"MOVING FORWARD" = WE'RE IGNORING THE PAST DISASTER

"PER MY LAST EMAIL" = CAN YOU READ

90. Permission Slips for Bad Work Days

-----✂---

Permission to leave at 5 PM without guilt

Your Signature: _____

-----✂---

Permission to say "I can't take that on"

Your Signature: _____

-----✂---

Permission to take a mental health day

Your Signature: _____

-----✂---

Permission to not respond after hours

Your Signature: _____

Permission to leave a job that's hurting you

Your Signature: _____

------✂--

Permission to prioritize yourself

Your Signature: _____

------✂--

Permission to be mediocre today

Your Signature: _____

------✂--

Permission to update your resume on your lunch break

Your Signature: _____

------✂--

Permission to stop caring so much

Your Signature: _____

91. Things You Don't Owe Your Job

- Your mental health
- Your physical health
- Your personal time
- Your relationships
- Your weekends
- Your passion
- Loyalty when they're not loyal back
- An explanation for taking PTO
- 24/7 availability
- Overwork to prove your worth
- Your entire personality
- Staying somewhere that makes you miserable

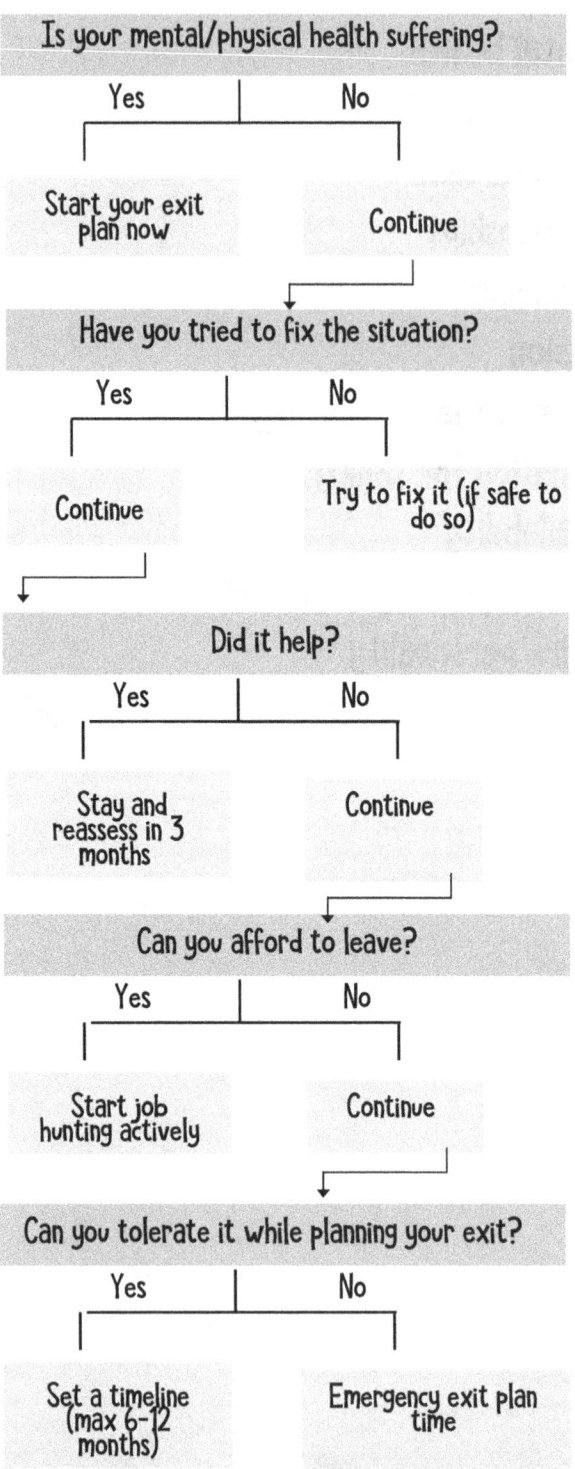

93. Tiny Wins Journal

When everything feels terrible, tiny wins count. Use the space below to jot down your tiny wins.

Today's tiny win: (Examples: Didn't cry. Took lunch. Said no to extra work. Updated resume. Made it through the day.)

One thing I'm proud of this week:

One boundary I set:

One thing I did for myself:

One reason I didn't quit today:

94. Burnout Checklist

You might be burnt out if:

- ☐ Everything feels overwhelming
- ☐ You can't focus or make decisions
- ☐ You're irritable with everyone
- ☐ You don't care about things you used to care about
- ☐ You're exhausted no matter how much you sleep
- ☐ You're getting sick more often
- ☐ You feel emotionally numb
- ☐ Small tasks feel impossible
- ☐ You fantasize about quitting constantly

If you checked 3+: You need rest, not a productivity app.

95. Things That Actually Help

- ☒ Therapy or counseling
- ☒ Walking during lunch breaks
- ☒ Setting actual boundaries
- ☒ Talking to someone who gets it
- ☒ Updating your resume (even if you're not leaving yet)
- ☒ Using your PTO
- ☒ Moving your body (even 10 minutes helps)
- ☒ Saying no more often
- ☒ Having a life outside work
- ☒ Remembering this is temporary
- ☒ Building an exit fund
- ☒ Connecting with people in your industry
- ☒ Learning new skills (for future you)

96. Things That Don't Help (But People Suggest Anyway)

- ✗ "Just think positive!"
- ✗ "At least you have a job"
- ✗ "Everyone deals with this"
- ✗ "You just need to work harder"
- ✗ "Have you tried yoga?" (Yoga is great. It's not a cure for toxic workplaces.)
- ✗ "You're so lucky"
- ✗ "Just quit if you're unhappy" (ignoring financial reality)
- ✗ "It'll get better eventually" (sometimes it won't)
- ✗ "You're too sensitive"
- ✗ "This is just part of adulting"

97. The Survival Mantra

One day at a time.

One meeting at a time.

One email at a time.

One breath at a time.

You don't have to conquer the whole week. Just get through today.

98. When to Get Professional Help

Please talk to someone if you're:

- Having regular panic attacks
- Unable to sleep (or sleeping way too much)
- Losing interest in everything
- Having thoughts of self-harm
- Using alcohol/substances to cope
- Feeling completely hopeless
- Struggling to get out of bed
- Experiencing physical symptoms (headaches, stomach issues, etc.)

Therapy isn't weakness. It's smart.

Your job is NOT worth your life.

National crisis lines exist. Use them if you need to.

99. You Survived Today

You made it.

Through the meeting that made you want to scream. The email that made your eye twitch. The moment you almost walked out and never came back.

You're still here.

That takes strength, even when it doesn't feel like it. Some days, survival IS the victory. And that's okay.

Tomorrow might be hard too. (Let's be honest, it probably will be.)

But you'll get through that one too. You always do.

100. This Isn't Forever

This job. This feeling. This moment.

None of it is permanent.

You won't feel this way forever. You won't be stuck forever. You won't be this tired forever.

Things will shift. Maybe not today. Maybe not next week. But eventually.

One day you'll look back on this time and realize how far you've come. How much you survived. How strong you actually are.

For now, just keep going.

One step. One day. One breath.

You've got this.

Especially when it doesn't feel like it.

When all else fails... repeat the following affirmations daily. Then color them if you dare.

Read This Again Later

You won't always feel ready—but you'll keep showing up anyway.

No one knows what they're doing.

Everyone's just improvising.

You're not lost—you're leveling up.

Keep choosing yourself. Keep laughing through the chaos.

You've got this—like, actually.

THE END

(Or really, just the beginning of whatever you choose next.)

www.ingramcontent.com/pod-product-compliance
Lightning Source LLC
Chambersburg PA
CBHW060804050426
42449CB00008B/1535